Healing the "Ouch" of Disappointment

by

Chlöe Asprey

Author Chlöe Asprey.

Illustrations by Marion Rhoades

First published in Great Britain 2013 by Forster Books.

Design and print by www.abbeyprinters.com

Copyright Chlöe Asprey.

Sponsored by Montessori St. Nicholas Charity.

All rights reserved. No part of this book may be reprinted or reproduced or utilised in any form without permission in writing from the publisher. The views and expressions in this book are of the author and cannot be attributed to Montessori.

Typeset in Palatino Linotype and Futura MD.

Chlöe is a grandmother, mother and wife
dividing her time between England and France.

She has travelled and worked all over the world
as a life coach/psychotherapist and is delighted
to share her experiences in this her first book.
She is also an artist and photographer.

www.chloeaspreyblog.com
www.tiegsolus.moonfruit.com

ANGELS ON THE SILK ROAD

*There are many truths and many paths
and so each day my journey starts.*

*Sometimes a moonbeam lingers on my brow,
Sometimes I am stirred by a promise from the sun,
Sometimes when I hear the dancing rain and wind I linger
and pretend it is still night,
Sometimes a young and gentle whisper will
entice me to arise.*

At times there are many tears that day – they are my journey too.

*Tears of joy, tears of laughter, tears of sorrow,
Tears of pain – sometimes, just tears.
As I taste the salt upon my lips, I remember I can drink the tears
to heal my wounds and thus have many gifts to offer and share with you.*

*There are times I am afraid as I descend down a path unknown
into the bowels of Mother Earth.
This journey is alone, there is no mortal you here.
From a yearning and a hunger to survive, to live, I do
battle, grapple with demons and hairy monsters.
Sometimes I bathe in the rich dark loam always with
a knowing I must die and in that death find a
lighted path ahead.*

*There are many teachers with many truths to guide and
divert me on my way.
Sometimes I listen, sometimes I sit at their feet,
sometimes I hear echoes from another time.
Sometimes I run away to play.
Sometimes I stare and cannot hear,
Sometimes I hear the voice within
and just as I think I know or disregard, I fall asleep
upon the path – wise fool and yet a teacher too.*

*There is a place upon the path, a place I love of
peace and ecstasy where Angels come and
take me to Great Mystery.*

by Chlöe Asprey

FOREWORD

I have known Chlöe for over 20 years, and in that time she has guided and counselled me through many a minor and major disappointment.

I don't believe it's useful to have regrets, and I believe one can try not to hold onto them. But disappointment is unavoidable, and to have the tools to recognise, deal with it, and accept it as part of life's rich pattern, is perhaps one of the most valuable of lessons we can learn.

In this book Chlöe shares her wisdom, her experience and her insight. It is a book to have and to give. This is not a self-help book; it is a book full of the wisdom of the ages and teaches important lessons that are relevant to all our lives.

Felicity Kendal.

DEDICATION

To all children, my sons and especially my precious grandchildren.

ACKNOWLEDGEMENTS

I would very much like to thank everyone who has contributed to this book. Without their stories the book wouldn't have happened. My very patient clients who have kept asking me about the book.

I would like to thank Karen Thornton and Claire Henshaw for the Bear Story Illustrations; Selina Baker and John Williams for their 30-Day Challenge which ensured my finishing the book.

I am incredibly grateful to Foster Books for agreeing to take on the publication of the book and to the Montessori St. Nicholas Charity whose principles are so relevant to nurturing and respecting every child's uniqueness.

I would like to thank my lovely proof-readers Jen and Judy, my family for supporting me and last but not least my precious grandchildren who were my inspiration and gave me that extra nudge to "get on with it". Of course my long suffering husband, David, who was disappointed on occasion by the scrappy meals I provided when in full flow!

CONTENTS

Introduction   13

Recognising Symptoms   17

Deconstructing Symptoms   21

Life's Disappointments   25

Forgiveness and Letting Go   28

Reclaiming our Confidence   32

Decoding and Cutting the Ties   36

Getting Disappointment to Work for You   39

Disappointment in Love   42

Creativity   45

Ceremony   51

Stress Management   55

Children   58

INTRODUCTION

Ever since I was a little girl I dreamed of going out bush with the Aboriginal people; in my forties all of a sudden this became a reality. My father and brother lived in Australia and one day my brother called me to say that my father was dying and could I come as soon as possible.

Within three days I was on a plane there. After my father sadly died, I found myself staying alone on my brother's land as he had disappeared for a few days to deal with his grief in his own way. One morning a friend of my brother's turned up and stayed for a cup of coffee. I told him that a while ago someone had told me I would find myself with an aboriginal tribe and that I had always had this as a dream when I was small.

Instead of looking at me as if I was delusional, he kindly explained that there were no Aboriginal people in Tasmania anymore and that I needed to go to Alice Springs. A few days later he arranged for me to travel there and gave me the number of a friend to call. As it so happened, the Aboriginal people found me and gave me instructions as to where to go, telling me I would spend time with one of their elders. As I had spent a lot of time with Native Americans I knew it was traditional to bring a gift for an elder. In the time I had before I set off, I wanted to take great care in preparing a gift.

I already had a very unusual crystal with me and I found a beautiful piece of cloth to wrap it in as well as a lovely basket just the right size. I spent hours meditating with it and making sure it was appropriate energetically.

The day came when I was to follow the directions I was given; a little nervous but very excited. One of my greatest dreams was about to come true. Finally I found myself sitting out in the wilderness in front of the elder of the tribe.

With great ceremony I handed over to her the little basket. There was a corner of the carefully chosen cloth peeking out and to my horror in an instant she had yanked the corner, the crystal flying out into the desert and her roaring with laughter.

I was SO disappointed. I wanted to cry and scream in anger at the same time. Bubbles of fear were coming up to the surface together with confusion. She continued to literally rock with laughter and eventually I just wanted to run away. Finally I looked up and saw that she had a quizzical look on her face as if to say "Now what are you going to do?" I felt that she could see right inside my whole being; nonetheless her eyes were still twinkling.

Then I heard myself say to myself "Well, you can't get a number 9 bus home, can you?" I finally understood the expression "disappointment takes a lot of planning". At last I saw the funny side of the whole thing, especially me. I got over myself and had one of the most life changing experiences ever, way beyond anything I could possibly have imagined.

In contrast to being able to laugh and turn the disappointment round, there are times when it is extremely painful. My mother, father and I all lived with my grandparents. When I was about 2, my mother became very ill and eventually, at about 3, I was sent away for a while. I missed my mother terribly and eventually I was told I would be going home. I was so excited and when we got there I rushed down the hall and burst into my parents' bedroom. The room was completely empty – bare floorboards, a bare light bulb hanging from the ceiling, no curtains and no furniture. All that was left was a row of my mother's shoes against a wall. She had died whilst I was away.

Today I know that the ball of feelings I felt were the symptoms of disappointment and subsequently grief. The effects of disappointment can feel like an actual bereavement and when that happens we need support. Sometimes if we bury our feelings, they colour what appear to be insignificant disappointments so that inexplicably you feel as if your heart is going to break.

Since being a grandmother and playing a part in little children growing up again, my desire to write this book has become stronger. As Daisaku Ikeda says in one of his meditation books "children are full of precious potential". Although this book on disappointment is for adults, the tools in it can also be passed on by example to children whether we are parents, extended family, godparents or teachers. There is also a specific section regarding children. We have a very rich pool of experience to share and we have all been children. There are many international organisations who care for the welfare of children and thank goodness that there are schools like Montessori which encourage their individuality and natural abilities. The extraordinary growth of these schools all over the world mirrors my own passion at a grass roots level to support these precious beings in the best way we can.

There are many levels of disappointment and the aim of this book is to help you identify them and be able to heal the ones you can. My experience is that support from good friends, family and, if necessary, professionals is an essential ingredient to the healing process regardless of the depth of disappointment. Hopelessness, isolation and hiding the feelings from others can be painful consequences of the confusion it creates.

We will look at ways you can identify disappointment and help you deconstruct the ball in order to deal with it in manageable ways using some of the suggested tools and most importantly finding your own workable tools. Interestingly, we can also explore the positive aspects of disappointment and how you can get it to work for you. There are also techniques that can help being more proactive and preventing disappointment taking its toll.

Before we start think of what disappointment means to you. The main definitions in English are: feeling of sadness or displeasure caused by non-fulfilment of hopes or expectations – deriving from Middle French meaning to remove from or deprive of an office or position.

In German it is: *enttäuschung* which means taking away a delusion or deception. In Arabic it means something along the lines of crushing hope - so harsh that you wouldn't dream of saying it to a child. In Danish it is: *aergelse* meaning resentment. What does the word mean to you personally, in your family or your culture?

Recognising Symptoms

In my own personal experience and as a psychotherapist/life coach disappointment can be a very painful combination of feelings and physical reactions. If left to fester like a buried wound, it can lead to feelings of betrayal and bitterness as well as despair, feeling unloved and abandoned. Not quite so simply dealt with by "pulling ourselves together", thinking of people worse off or having someone say to you "well, it's obvious isn't it, it's about expectations and boosting our self-worth".

As I mentioned before, recognising the symptoms of disappointment is the first step in healing the effects. Once we can identify them, we can then deconstruct them.

When I ask people what happens to them when they are disappointed they often say they either feel angry or sad, or then begin to feel confused because they can then feel more than one response. The following are exercises to help begin this process. I suggest that you do this gently and in stages rather than do all of it at once. Keeping a journal during this process can be really helpful. Here is an example of how to journal:

The following questions can be used as a format for the journal:
- What have I learned?
- What was useful to me?
- What was not useful to me?
- How can I apply what I have learned to my life?

- What have I experienced emotionally, physically, mentally, spiritually?
- What do I need to know more about?
- What action do I need to take?

For some people it is easier to start with these questions and that is all they need to do. For others it is easier to simply write how they are feeling (conscious streaming) or tell the story on one side of a journal and then pick out salient points or answer the above questions on the other side of the journal. This second method is a useful tool to identify patterns of reaction, either of acceptance or rejection of information.

Sometimes the information that initially did not appear to be useful may then become so or it may trigger self-direction (i.e. this isn't helpful but I have remembered some old information which is). Sometimes it is helpful to switch methods to avoid assumptions.

In order to start recognising your symptoms, you can either look through the following examples and see if you can identify with them or sit quietly and think of a time when you were really disappointed or someone was disappointed in you. You may literally feel the symptoms again or simply observe them. If you can, gently scan your body and see where/how you were affected **physically:**

- Is there a feeling in the pit of your stomach?
- Is there a sense of holding back tears?
- Is there a sensation in your throat?
- Is your chest hurting?
- Does your throat or chest feel hot?
- Do you want to run?
- Do you want to break something?
- Do you want to lash out?
- What else ....?

If we can begin to define the symptoms physically, we become more aware of them beginning to happen and they can work like an "early warning system" so that we don't tumble into a vortex of feelings.

Again sitting quietly, notice what was happening to you **emotionally.** Are you feeling:

- Angry?
- Sad?
- Angry and sad?
- Guilty – I should be grateful?
- Ashamed – I shouldn't be feeling like this?
- Frightened?
- Resentful?
- Ungrateful?
- Hopeless?
- What else ....?

Sometimes our first response can be that our brain feels numb, so what are the **mental** symptoms?

- Do you actually try to stop thinking?
- Do you start to speak to yourself, running conversations in your head?
- Do you go over and over the situation until it becomes a pre-occupation?
- Do you find it difficult to concentrate?
- Do you tell yourself to pull yourself together?
- What else ....?

Disappointment can also affect us **spiritually:**

- Do you lose trust and faith in yourself?
- Do you lose trust and faith in the spiritual practice you may have?
- Do you feel there must be something different about you because other people seem to trust and have faith?
- Do you isolate and begin to feel "what is the point of it all"?
- Do you feel abandoned?
- What else ....?

Now that you are beginning to identify your personal responses to disappointment, think of a key incident in your life where you know you were deeply disappointed or someone was disappointed in you. How is this affecting your life today? Does it affect how you think, feel and react to certain situations? Is it a bit like Pavlov's dog, a bell (trigger) rings and you tumble back into some old feelings/responses? One of mine is "you of all people, I am surprised". There is still an "ouch" if I am feeling vulnerable or simply tired. However, I recognise it today and can step back from it fairly quickly.

If you can't think of anything right now, just imagine what might affect you in the future, or do you avoid certain situations so as not to be triggered? Reflect on how disappointment has affected relationships with other people? Are there certain relationships that it affects more than others? These can be with authority figures in general, parents or teachers. It can affect how we choose friends, lovers, partners in business or people to support us.

Disappointing experiences can influence how we respond to places and objects. Again take some time to think about what decisions you have made in your life based on these symptoms. Maybe re-read everything that you have written down and begin to think of the situations that you dealt with well as well as ones that still cause you that "ouch" feeling.

Deconstructing Symptoms

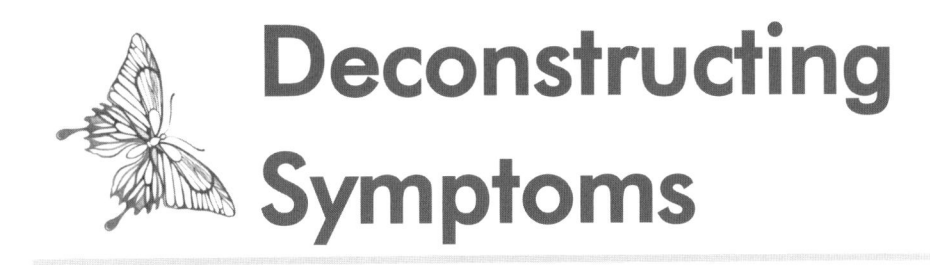

One of the ways you can deconstruct symptoms is by telling the story of an event which you now recognise as being about disappointment. Chantal's story is a good example and Queen Mary Syndrome has become part of my disappointment terminology.

Chantal's Story

France, Christmas 2006. We had just urged the plumber to stop drilling holes through our walls and to go home and prepare for his own seasonal celebrations. I felt mentally and physically exhausted. Not well disposed to cooking festive meals in dusty surroundings with metres of unconnected pipes hanging out of gaping holes in my kitchen walls. But at the back of my mind was a cheering thought, burning like a midnight candle – escape from Maison DIY and have the chance to see family and friends. We arranged to fly to the UK after Christmas. Last minute decision to touch base with all our loved ones at this special time of year.

The morning of December 29th came. After a day of meticulous preparation, in high spirits, the house was locked up, the cats entrusted to our lovely French neighbours and we were on our way.

Carcassonne airport was busy – people milling around carrying gift-wrapped parcels and small children clutching cuddly toys. There was an unmistakable buzz of happy people chatting and very soon I was also projecting myself into the visits and family gatherings we'd planned for our short break. Before I knew it, it was our turn to check in. I handed over our passports and then heard the Ryanair girl behind the desk ask my husband if he had another passport. Of course he hadn't. What an odd question!

Then came the blow...his passport was out of date and he would not be allowed to board the plane.

My mind did a somersault...everything I was looking forward to suddenly reappeared before my eyes and simultaneously disappeared down a long passage. My husband was dumbstruck and looked sad. It took all my self-control not to hurl abuse at him. Ryanair staff were giving out information about emergency passports and how to get hold of them. Nothing was going on in my head. The emergency was right here and now. I was being torn in two. I was launched to go, already in the UK, our French home far behind. How could I contemplate not going? The minutes that followed seemed like an eternity as I held on to the idea of boarding the plane alone, while knowing as I looked at my husband's wounded expression that I would not board alone...

A tumult of emotions overwhelmed me. I walked away from the departure area and in the comparative privacy of the rental car office, I burst into tears. Tears of frustration and disappointment.... so much disappointment .. .a feeling of hurt for which there is no balm and little acknowledgement ...a lump of unresolved emotion with nowhere to go, sitting like a stone in my heart. **The Queen Mary**, *after a monumental build-up of steam to prepare for sailing, on the point of nosing out of the port, was being asked to reverse and return to anchor. Not an easy task.*

The following days saw me descend into a dark place; my suitcase stood packed in my kitchen, a constant reminder of my disappointment. My husband got into his work clothes and resumed his DIY tasks in silence, seemingly unperturbed. His normal behaviour alienated me increasingly; I sought refuge in the support and understanding of my ever-loving girlfriends. Then I saw a way to turn the **Queen Mary** *round. I would go to the UK and it would be an enjoyable experience. Tickets on the net for early January were still cheap, so I booked flights to travel with a dear girlfriend, who is a close neighbour in France. Suddenly all seemed possible again and with a few phone calls I'd salvaged some of our aborted plans and regained confidence in the world.*

On this trip I had more time to relax and I was able to visit my elderly and sick mother, which had been one of my greatest concerns. I returned to France a much happier woman. Ultimately a change in timing proved to be positive, though I can't say that it was a painless experience. Disappointment is a bitter pill to swallow.

The lesson is probably something to do with letting go of outcome, trusting in life and not getting stuck in the **Queen Mary Syndrome!**

Once you have written the story, begin to look at the language you have used. The Queen Mary was a huge ocean-going liner which already sets the scene for the story. Her build-up towards flying to England is quite dramatic: **urged, exhausted, burning like a midnight candle, all our loved ones, special time of year, meticulous preparation, high spirits.** She then acknowledges she was projecting herself into the future. The combination of language and projecting was beginning to run a colourful scenario in her head which in turn would stimulate an array of emotions.

Next she describes the incident that provokes the disappointment and notice how she describes that as a blow. Following this come the symptoms; interestingly her initial response is mental: my mind did a somersault. Then the mental, physical, emotional started to mix in together. Her sense of time changed: the minutes that followed seemed like an eternity. Finally the feeling of 'overwhelm' happened. She can then really identify the disappointment and that it feels as if there is no balm; **a lump of unresolved emotion with nowhere to go, sitting like a stone in my heart.** Sometimes disappointment can literally feel as if your heart is breaking. Although she cried she wasn't able to unravel her emotions for a while and interestingly she left her packed suitcase where she could constantly see it.

Eventually she was able to reach out to her support system of friends including a friend accompanying her on her eventual trip to England which had a positive outcome. By stepping back and identifying the different stages of her disappointment she could see that letting go of outcomes, trusting in life and not getting stuck in the Queen Mary syndrome would be helpful in her not experiencing the bitter pill of disappointment.

It is important to stress that this is not about putting a dampener on plans but to be aware of climbing into the event in technicolour before it has actually happened. The Queen Mary herself was so massive that she needed several tug boats to guide her in and out of port. These can represent a metaphor for easing yourself in and out of situations. Disappointment can also come about from having had such **an amazing time** and coming back to our normal lives can be painful if we don't let the tug boats do their work. I know I have experienced this quite a few times in my life and can be quite unpleasant to be around and then have added guilt about my behaviour to the mix. I certainly have enough battle scars to have learned to prepare for re-entry.

Life's Disappointments

Disappointment can also come about from what I call "life disappointments". Natural dreams have just not materialised; as Luna describes it: "the ordinary part of the fabric of life".

Luna's story

I am half of an unexplained infertility couple, with nine years of wondering, relaxing, trying not to try, then investigations, waiting, poor management of treatment (never knowing what was on offer and what we should push for), acupuncture, homeopathy, group work, my own art psychotherapy practice....then going private to do the last cycle and feeling genuinely cared for. But, when it didn't work they offered us more. I was 39 by then and had thought "God preserve me from still trying at 40". One fertility doctor said to me, as if a consolation for not having a baby "they do grow up you know". How could he not grasp that the disappointment was not having kids growing up, to be a nuisance, to get mad at, to worry about, to be the ordinary part of the fabric of life.

A clairvoyant I visited for guidance said something useful, that it could not be put behind me but beside me. These children who filled our imaginary lives were probably out there somewhere, just not with us.

So we went off round the world, we got on with living life and on return I began to take my work seriously for the first time in ten years. Ceremony helped too. We had buried some of our disappointments under the raspberries, others were floated off to the sea. I ran workshops for other

*people about this coping process, I felt quite balanced about it.
I was not prepared for an unexpected pregnancy at 47, and yet another early miscarriage. This disappointment was a deep sharp grief, and one I could not so easily share with my husband. We spun off in different directions, and I took my disappointment into a crazy affair with someone who also wanted another late child... to cover their disappointment that they had somehow missed their two children's early lives.*

Well I got through the chaos. I became suddenly ill, and perhaps that pulled us to our senses. We got married after all, after 27 years I was seriously ill for about four years, which brought in a sudden menopause, facing the final end of hope. I am now very dependent on drug therapy, but managing life, savouring it. It's possible this chronic illness is what contributed to infertility, yet these continual experiences of disappointment helped me to manage disability, and I have had an outlook of making the best of things which I don't think I would have had without the setbacks for that part of my "fertile" years.

There remains the overlapping pain of seeing other people's grandchildren arrive. Even at age 30, for some reason I had known this was the part I would miss, envy at the sheer delight, the fierce and all the more unconditional love for one's children's children...and the sense of the generations going on, making meaning of life.

We have been out for the day today, a bank holiday, full of children everywhere, and we still ponder our empty car which once was full of the ghosts of the little ones arguing in the back... quieter now, grown up and away. The disappointment doesn't go away, it changes, and sits pale beside me like a transparent shadow... waxing and waning like the phases of the moon, but enriching me with its reflected light.

Luna's story reflects the well trodden path of the grief process. It can come about through any form of loss and letting go. Bizarrely even as a result of a positive change in our lives. The feelings of joy and

loss of the familiar can collide with each other and as my husband says we can then become disappointed that we are disappointed. However hard we might try to avoid it, it happens. As you might know there are clearly defined stages:
- Shock, feeling numb
- Anger: sometimes at self, sometimes at others, sometimes both
- Bargaining: if only .....
- Searching to replace what has been lost
- Sadness
- Acceptance

Luna works her way through this process until she arrives at an acceptance that gives her comfort. Acceptance can be the last stage but Melody Beattie in her book The Grief Club writes about how it can lead beyond that to enlightenment. The most painful aspect of grief is when we deny its existence or become stuck in one of the first five stages.

A lighter example is: We decide to have a delicious cup of tea before going out, but it is too hot and we need to add some cold water to make it drinkable, some of the "delicious tea" has to be poured out in order to make room. This appears to be a fairly straightforward solution. However, fear of losing the deliciousness and being late can cause us to either burn our mouths or pour the tea away incurring even more disappointment and loss.

Forgiveness and Letting Go

George's Story

As a kid, my brother Gary was 7 years younger than me. He was a lovely little kid and we got on very well together. I was always there for him, but as we grew up we grew apart through our pasts and addictions. Mostly on my part, then all on my part but my brother never gave up. I would tell him to 'f off' and I never wanted to see him again and that I would hurt him if he kept coming round. My Julie answered the phone one day many years after and it was my brother Gary asking if he could see me. I said no and to tell him I wanted nothing to do with him. After the conversation had finished, Julie come to me and said he was dying and would I give him the time of day. I had to chew this over for some time. My Julie would say it would be a nice thing to do so I agreed. My Julie phoned my brother and told him that I would see him, she said he was over the moon. When my brother first came round it was very very difficult for me to show any worth, I had nothing to give. My words were just words, empty words. It would have been so easy to say 'f off' but I didn't. As time went on we got to know one another again, we started to laugh and become much closer. I could see he was very ill, he was dying of cancer and had lost so much weight, lumps and bumps were coming up all over him. I agreed for him to stay for one weekend. He was like that little kid I once remembered, he did not stop singing and was trying to dance. He was so high he never slept.

When we were saying our goodbyes standing on my outside steps I couldn't help it, I hugged my brother for the very first time in my life and I could feel his bones. When I stepped back and looked at him, his eyes had welled up and tears had started to run down his cheeks - he did have lovely big brown eyes. He thanked me and I saw him round to his car. I had been looking after my brother with a few quid and was glad to do so. As my brother got into his car and turned the key, knowing I was all soft and soppy after our hug, he looked at me with those big brown eyes and said "I am not so sure I'll make it back bruv, I am a bit short of petrol". The crafty little monkey, but I just had to bung him a few more quid. Not too long after my brother died, it's hard to describe how I really felt, it was not good. I missed him. I missed him a lot more than I probably showed. As soon as I woke he was there, I would talk to him every day but I was so very glad that we had that precious time together, so very glad.

Lizzy's story

When I was about five, I remember standing by the front door with my coat on waiting to "go up to London to see the Christmas lights". I don't think I knew what that meant but I had been told that it was exciting and a reward of some kind. Suddenly, my mother told us that we weren't going because we had been naughty. I felt crushed, as if I had been hit by a hammer and like a wave, a huge wave of something black came up from inside me and overwhelmed me with feelings I couldn't name or begin to explain. I know now that those feelings are disappointment.

I have been working through these childhood memories and feelings and forgiveness of my Mum has helped me to feel compassion for her in that situation. I now understand that the enormity of her fears (whatever they were) was such that she had to disappoint a small child rather than face them.

I have put these two stories together because they are very different and yet George and Lizzy arrive at the same place of acceptance, able to let go. One of the most important things I have learned over the years is "it is not what other people (or life experiences) do to me, it is what I do with them". When I hold onto blame, including blaming myself, I lose my freedom and disconnect from the world around me, particularly people. A sense of shame and guilt can start to worm into our psyches attaching itself to other sources of disappointment. If George had carried on blaming himself for his behaviour he would never have had that precious time with his brother.

Although her mother was no longer alive Lizzy got to a place of compassion by forgiving her mother. Forgiveness in this case is about reconnection not about feeling superior and condescending. We can have a visceral reaction to the word forgiveness perhaps connected to experiences where we have felt patronised. This is not about disempowering ourselves, but rather about taking responsibility. Somebody asked me the question "It's OK to feel that way, but how long do you want to feel like that for?"
We are definitely entitled to our feelings but nursing and nurturing them can be even more painful. Sometimes like a dog we can bury them like a bone and dig them up every now and again to see if there is any meat left on the bone.

How do we let go? I think the first step is about being willing to be willing to let go. Like George "chewing it over" or like Lizzy getting some support to work through the memories. Sometimes writing a letter to the person if they have died and then burning it.
If the resentments are strong the letter can start from there but keep going until something clears. I am a great believer in doing something physically, so it could be throwing a stone into the sea or a river representing your willingness to let go. Burning a list of resentments or self blame is another suggestion. Find your own way of doing something physical – your body remembers taking the action.

There is a Jewish expression that if you start walking on the path, God will meet you half way. There is a Buddhist practice called Deep Sange where you chant in order to clear the karma around these situations. In 12-Step programmes like Alcoholics Anonymous working the steps can help you find resolution. These are a few of the ways we can do this. Therefore it feels like a given that we will have these issues and that we can resolve them.

Reclaiming our Confidence

Tom's Story

I had been working in the same place for several years and was, frankly, getting bored. The people in charge of the business had left and been replaced with far less qualified and less experienced individuals who had very little interest in staff morale or decent customer service. I was on the verge of handing in my notice when I found out that someone I knew was planning to buy the company and run it himself. He was familiar with the way I worked and was keen for me to still be in place within the business should his takeover be successful. So I bit my tongue and bided my time and put up with everything that was going on under the current owners, and any time I was down or frustrated I told myself how good it would be once the new regime took over.

Nearly two years later, after a number of false dawns and failed bids, I finally had to accept that the one thing I was waiting for was never going to happen.

The disappointment was crushing.

I'd wasted two years hanging on in the hope of better times and now, not only was I having to face up to the fact that I was going to have to leave for the sake of my own sanity and health, I was also having to start the process TWO YEARS LATER than I might have done.

It was very, very tough to pick myself up and get my confidence back. The job market was in a much trickier state than it had been previously and quite a few people I knew who had left the company in the intervening years

were struggling for work, and for money. I started doubting whether leaving was ever a good idea in the first place, and allowed myself to believe that whatever I might choose to do instead, it was bound to end in just another disappointment.
It would take me close to another two years before I would finally recover enough to resign....

Tom's story is not unusual. He describes his disappointment as crushing and sometimes we are afraid to move forward after experiencing such strong emotions. We can feel trapped between what happened and avoiding what might happen again.

When we lose our confidence we can become frozen and unable to make the changes we would like to. Reclaiming our lost self becomes vital and very often we need help with this either professionally or from trusted friends and family. Writing out our strengths and expertise is one way of starting this process, following it up by talking it through with other people. Our thinking can become confused and we can tend to see the glass half empty instead of half full and when we are in this place we can become members of the "Aint it Awful Club" or as Caroline Myss says "bonding on the wound", attracting other people in the same predicament. Initially this can be comforting and takes away the isolation but then reinforces staying stuck. In some extreme cases we can wear our pain like a badge of honour and allow it to become our identity.

Sometimes you need to check out the truth. For instance you might be telling yourself that work is hard to find – so challenge this by asking yourself: is this REALLY REALLY true, is this PARTIALLY true, or is this NOT TRUE AT ALL. When we lose our confidence, we can tend to go into "self-fulfilling prophecy" mode. When I was contemplating going back to work after having had children, I lost my confidence and someone helped me look at all the transferable organisational skills I had and how I was used to managing the unexpected, balancing different people's needs etc.

Losing our confidence can be described as losing heart or losing our spirit. Many spiritual practices have ceremonies where you literally call your spirit back, as it is understood that our spirit/our soul can jump out of our body during deep trauma. In the western world we can more readily accept this when people are under anaesthetic and share about floating above their bodies during an operation or in near death experiences. The turmoil of deep emotions can have the same effect. Therefore calling your spirit back can be a very powerful way of reclaiming your spirit, your vital force. Sitting somewhere quietly and saying out loud that you want your lost spirit back is a way of putting out your willingness for this to happen. Writing a letter to the Universe and asking for it back and posting it to yourself is another way. If you have a specific religious practice and going to your place of worship and lighting a candle or praying is yet another way. It is strongly advised, once you have put out the willingness, to undertake this within a safe environment.
In the early part of his story, Tom describes the symptoms of being stuck really well. A tool that can help with this is a simple exercise which is a form of vision setting.

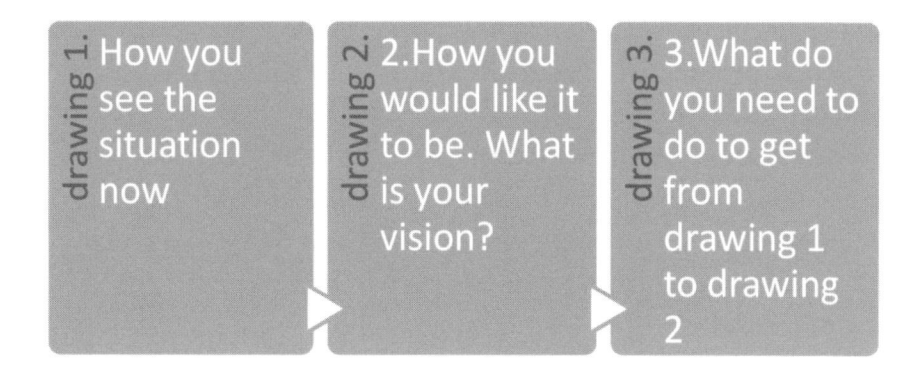

| drawing 1. How you see the situation now | drawing 2. 2.How you would like it to be. What is your vision? | drawing 3. 3.What do you need to do to get from drawing 1 to drawing 2 |

Although this is not about how good the drawings are, you may prefer to use words instead. If answers don't come immediately, it can help to put the first two drawings up somewhere and reflect or meditate on them until you can see what you can do about the situation. Allow other people to see them. Children very often spot the obvious before we do. Out of the mouths of babes....

Decoding and Cutting the Ties

Michael's story

I was born in 1935 in London and after experiencing the horrors of the Blitz in 1941 I was evacuated to South Wales, returning to my family in 1945. During my time away I saw my mother once and did not see my father until my return home.

Due to an exceptional singing (boy treble) voice, I won a place at a good London Grammar School. During my time at this school I struggled academically. However, I exceeded at extracurricular activities:

- *As a singer I sang as a soloist at the Royal Albert Hall on three occasions and many other leading concert halls.*
- *I was Cox of the school "Rowing Eight" competing in the 'Head of the River Race' - this takes place the day before the Boat Race.*
- *As a swimmer I competed as a High Board Diver winning several important school and club level competitions.*

I weighed less than 6 stone stone yet competed in the London School Boy Boxing Championship and with the help of two wins arrived at the Royal Albert Hall for the finals. My match finished in approximately 20 seconds when the referee stopped the action. I was physically sick, my nose was bleeding and I was crying.

My father never heard me sing, never saw me cox the boat, never saw me dive. YET he was there at my boxing disaster. He put his arm around me and said "Well done son, now you are a man".

It took a long time for me to know that it is best to succeed than to lose despite my father's judgement But once I had learned that, it has been a very good life and I have enjoyed success and handled failure well.

Michael's story is about cutting the inappropriate ties with his father, i.e his judgement of what makes a man. Another way of cutting the ties is decoding. There is a book called "Cutting the Ties that Bind" by Phyllis Krystal that is extremely helpful and suggests different ways we can do this.

For instance, we can visualize the ties being dissolved and I always suggest that the ends are cauterised with unconditional love. Another way is step into a sacred fire and ask for them again to be dissolved. Imagine standing under a waterfall and imagine them being washed away. You can reinforce this when you have a shower and watch the water go down the plug hole. Have a bath with some cleansing essential oils and again watch the water drain away. A cold dip in the sea is another way. Using incense and particularly Native American smudge is a very efficient way of clearing energy.

Here are some thoughts from clients who have put this into action:

Sarah

I would want to do this if I have been in a situation where I had felt uncomfortable or overwhelmed, good or bad or where I was getting flashbacks to past events without consciously trying to recall them. I find the benefits to be very grounding. It enables me to connect with my higher power in a clearer way. It makes me feel clean and lighter.

Why might we resist? I would resist doing it if I was too responsible for a person and I felt they needed me (I am not saying this is the right thing to do but subconsciously I do it sometimes).

Why might it be a difficult concept to take on board? At first I thought I might feel isolated and lonely by doing it and it would leave me feeling raw and empty; now I know it makes me feel more complete.

Diane

I want to do this to be free, make clear judgements, stay calm – if not problems get out of control and I lose perspective.

Why would I resist? Sometimes it feels easier to stay in the same territory, might be scary to see it from the outside. Afraid I might lose control if I was totally detached. Somehow I can enjoy being angry – this is what I have discovered.

It is sometimes difficult to take on board because we are all creatures of habit as well as copying others (a sense of belonging). However I understand that we need to erase certain memories/concepts and start afresh.

Catherine

I had to cut the ties with my daughter's outburst because it was twisting my gut. It hurt and seemed so unfair. It meant sitting down and working out that within what she said there was some truth, isolating that from how I had been drawn into the drama when I couldn't pause to think. If I hadn't cut the ties I would have accumulated a load of negativity and emotionally we would have gone round in circles. I can't afford to be that angry and I need to stay focused.

I recognise that I used to enjoy getting angry and that it gave me a false sense of being in control. Now it is about me being as clean as I can be energetically without being priggish.

It can take a long time to realise that we are corded on in the first place and like Michael it can take time. One of the ways I describe the benefits is to think of a tumble dryer and how much better it works if we remember to defluff it and avoid the risk of it catching fire.

Getting Disappointment to Work for You

Frank's story

When I was younger I got the "programming" from well-meaning people around me that I should pursue a "good solid career" (in my case in computer science) rather than going for it with my "hobbies" (music and drama at the time)...
The "advice" I got was along the lines of "you'll always have your hobbies to enjoy in your spare time, but if you try and make a living out of them, even though you're good, you won't make any money ... unless you have a lot of luck...and also they won't be hobbies any more, so you probably won't enjoy them as much (?!?!?!?)"

So of course I pursued the "solid career" and did what was expected of me. The "expectation" wasn't heavy or consciously forced; however, I was brought up "not to let people down" as an important value... and of course I transferred this into my early career choices!!

I've kept up with the music (piano player, do a bit of composing and recording .. both my children are learning instruments... so music still very much part of life... as a hobby!)
Drama... kept going with this until my mid-20s in various theatre groups/university etc ... did a whole range of acting - even a tiny bit on TV!! (fluky and unaccredited :-).... but dropped it all when "career" got busy and then family etc... maybe I'll tread the boards again one day.. maybe it was something for then... I don't know... we'll see...

What is interesting is that Frank didn't stop keeping his hobbies alive and has passed that pleasure on to his children. He has also left the corporate world and become self-employed which is about following his heart. I asked him to give me a story about disappointment and so there was an element of that in "programming" but he has got that to work for him not against him. He still feeds his soul with what he likes doing and he has left the door open to other possibilities "maybe I'll tread the boards again"..........

Leo's Story

I was in my early twenties and had been headhunted directly from University into the hotel industry which had been my dream ever since I was about nine years old. I joined the management programme provided by a major hotel chain which was an amazing opportunity and privilege.

I found myself early on in my second assignment in a fun city. When I got my final appraisal I was told that they were really disappointed in my performance after all the special training and opportunities I had received. My initial reaction was "Well if that is the case, I will go elsewhere". However, in my heart of hearts I knew that it was a true comment as I had been cocky and was enjoying the city a little too much. It was the first time in my life I had had real negative feedback on my performance.

It brought me back down to earth and I made a commitment to turn things around. I managed to do this quite quickly and, to my surprise, the feedback I then got from them was that in fact they respected me more that I turned things around than if I had just carried on doing a good job. Ten years later I am still with the same company and hopefully have not forgotten the lesson about getting cocky thanks to being told I had disappointed them.

Leo is in fact my son and typing his story out and the fact that he has given me permission brings tears to my eyes. In life, we will inevitably come to a time when we will get negative feedback. Many spiritual teachings and personal development techniques tell us to "expect nothing" and sometimes I think that it can be a form of avoidance of disappointment. This can become more about resignation rather than acceptance; perhaps even a way to stifle our dreams and ambitions. It can become a form of control. If I hadn't stepped outside of my comfort zone, I would never have written this book.

Admitting that we have gone through the process of being disappointed can be really useful. It can flush up some negative strategies we have developed. When I first started working on this I saw a pattern around my giving people gifts. I call this pattern "gilding the lily". I would genuinely give someone a gift from my heart and then I would put an extra special ribbon round it. It had absolutely nothing to do with making the gift look attractive – it was the process in my head that was so subtle, together with a physiological change in my body as I tied the ribbon. It came from a deep-seated thought that the gift might not be good enough and would disappoint the person or even worse that it would help me avoid seeing their disappointment. It would be great if this never happened now but at least I recognise the symptoms and can stop myself, look at what might be behind this behaviour. The deconstruction process and recognising the symptoms can be great tools in stopping us going into old, unhelpful behaviours.

Perfectionism is often a symptom of avoiding disappointment and making mistakes. One of the uncomfortable aspects of perfectionism is that we have to come out of denial to recognise it. One of the ways we might be challenged into doing this is when other people say to you "Wow, I don't know how you do it? I couldn't." This is not necessarily a compliment. It can be very useful to ask yourself "How do I do it". What price are you paying? How stressed are you? Is this how you get your brownie points? This is not about doing well, this is about overdoing it. Most of us want to do the best we can - this is about going out of kilter. There are some stress management tools later on in the book which can also flush this up...

I need to remind myself that practically all the most exciting inventions in the world came about through mistakes! Think about it. Another reminder for me is the beautiful rainbows in clear quartz crystals. They actually come from imperfections within the crystal. Absolutely perfect imperfection.

Disappointment *in* Love / Unrequited Love

Hundreds and thousands of poets, musicians, writers, film makers, and singers have imbued our lives with tales of unrequited love. Journals and diaries can bulge with sad stories of disappointment and hurt. It can almost feel like a badge of honour to have the scars from it. Rooms echo and reverberate from the pain of its disclosure. The intensity of the descriptions mirror the very real feelings people experience. In its extreme people will drink, take drugs, overeat, starve, put themselves at risk and at worst commit suicide.

These feelings can run through a family's DNA and create warnings about "whatever you do, don't expect too much". Sometimes unresolved issues of abandonment in childhood can make us either needy or commitment-phobic which will simply reinforce the feelings of abandonment. We can also stay in a fantasy world where we don't risk being abandoned and therefore are separated from the outside world. This doesn't just happen to women. I see both men and women and as I am writing this am thinking about two young thirty-something men who are extremely successful at work, and on the outside have everything going for them. Yet as a result of unrequited love in their teenage years they have responded to the disappointment in a painful way. Meeting them you would have no idea because the issues were so deeply buried. One has commitment issues and the other has simply created a wall around him so as not to be hurt. Fortunately they are both aware of the consequences and are willing to work through this in order to have a complete life for themselves. Imagine what happens when a couple meet who have similar hidden wounds and enter into a relationship.

Notice me, choose me, show me that you love me – are these familiar thoughts/behaviours? "I will make myself as attractive as possible" and then we don't understand why it doesn't work, then we go into shame, low self-worth and disappointment sets in. All this can reinforce a core belief that we are unloveable.

Martha's story

I started Internet dating and there was this man. At first it was exciting, a good-looking guy, an interesting profile and the thrill that he kept viewing me. After a short time, if he viewed me I had a good day and if he didn't, I didn't.
When I eventually discovered that he wasn't real but a photo of a model and a profile constructed by a con artist I was devastated. I felt empty, stupid and full of shame.

Sadly Martha's story is not unusual. Fortunately she found out the con and it has taken her to a place where she is working on her abandonment issues – nonetheless a painful way to get there.

A friend reminded me of a Diane Keaton film made in the late 70s called Looking for Mr. Goodbar. The story is about a young teacher whose first love is an affair with an older man and he ends it. She already has body images due to a serious scar on her back. She feels used and reacts by picking up men on one-night stands whilst maintaining a vocational job working with deaf children. She sees her night prowls as a way of providing excitement in her apparently ordinary life.

Then she puts herself more and more at risk and although she meets someone who is looking for a normal relationship, she turns it down. In the end she decides she has had enough and has one more pick-up before she stops and sadly she ends up being killed by this last man. This film is based on a true story and now, 36 years later, the Internet has made taking these risks much easier and more dangerous. You can sit at home and cruise and no one need know.

As Martha said, it can influence what kind of day you have – a very powerful drug. Being killed still happens and I have a friend whose partner was killed by meeting someone on the Internet because they thought the grass might be greener somewhere else.

How do we heal this kind of disappointment? It takes time and very often professional help. Often we need to go back to the original abandonment and heal that first. Then gently rebuild our self-worth. One way is to begin to nurture ourselves, and I mean nurture not self-indulge which can simply cover over the issues and in a strange way make us more unhappy when it doesn't change the way we feel inside. Sometimes asking ourselves the question "What would I do for someone I really loved?" and do it for ourselves. "What would my ideal relationship look like?" Can I provide some of those things for myself?

Nurturing ourselves, our soul, and not the wounds, is very important. This is somewhere where bonding on the wound is very detrimental. Joining the "I hate men/women" club will keep us stuck. Find out how other people have recovered well from unrequited love or disappointments in love. Neuro-Linguistic Programming (NLP) can also be helpful as it changes the negative pictures in our head and replaces them with positive ones. This is very different from pasting over the negative with fantasy.

Having healing treatments can be very helpful as they are usually not about talking but about allowing ourselves to receive some gentle and loving care. Be kind and thoughtful to you. Notice who are your friends and people who genuinely smile at you. As it was pointed out to me we need to flourish not just survive. Connecting with others is part of that.

Creativity

How to use creativity when we are disappointed? Well in a lot of teachings, creativity is our vital force, our oomph which fuels our lives. A few years ago I had the opportunity to spend some time with the Alcohol and Drug Unit in Alice Springs who worked with the Aboriginal people communities.

As an act of desperation, the grandmothers of certain tribes got together to see if they could find an effective way of helping the children who remained in the communities and help heal their own disappointment at what had happened to their families. These children were turning more and more to petrol sniffing to alleviate their inner turmoil. Many of the mothers had turned to prostitution and the fathers to alcoholism. This situation is not unique to the aboriginals and is mirrored all over the world.

Painting was something the children could relate to, as selling paintings to tourists and collectors was a way of making money. The traditional symbols were still being used as they appealed to tourists.

The grandmothers knew that if they tackled the situation head on with the children they too would end up like their parents. What they decided to do was paint apparently for themselves. The grandmothers gathered together and used anything to paint with and on.

They banked on the fact that the children might still be curious. The grandmothers just carried on painting and slowly the children began to sit with them and pick up brushes and copy their grandmothers. The grandmothers would start to explain the stories behind the symbols they painted. They also showed the children in the paintings what was happening to their brains by sniffing petrol. In this way they combined painting and storytelling and the healing process began to take hold. These projects have expanded and some of the parents have started to come back to the communities because of the changes in their children. I spent time with children who had experienced this healing and they were happy and contented as children are when they feel safe. It has been an everlasting source of inspiration for me and a great reminder of the healing that takes place through creativity.

Avrum's poem

Ship in Turmoil
The ship was tossed, thrown from side to side
The wind harassed the ship,
Sending the wheel on an everlasting spin.
The wind howling, billowing, shrieking like a car breaking
As I strained to turn the writhing boat,
I was thrown by the hand of the wind.
Thrown to shore like a ball against a wall.
The destruction of the wind ceased to thrive.
My molested boat was wrecked beyond salvation

Avrum is also my son and when he wrote this he was 14 and life was tough, his father was incredibly ill and Avrum's life was constantly disrupted by visits to the hospital to say goodbye to his father. His father was a little bit like Lazarus and would rally round, only to go back into hospital again. Avrum's feelings were overwhelming at times and writing this poem helped him to express those feelings openly. It helped his school and me to understand the depth of his feelings. Deep down he was also disappointed at how his teenage years were full of sadness and fear. He has continued to use his creativity well and is now a very gifted chef.

Daniel's Story

What's in a name?
So, she was pregnant, and of course, I'd do the right thing. Filled with a mixture of fear and trepidation, I simply took my courage into my hands and I decided right there and then: "I'll support whichever decision you make; it's your body." She replied, with tears streaming down her pretty face, "OK then, I'll do it: we'll have a baby".

Months passed as we got to know each other a bit better, the details of a hurried, strange and unfamiliar contract. We began to learn about the rough with the smooth, the unexpected flinty, sharp bits and the unexplorable, darker memories of another past and funny stuff and sad stuff: regrets and in the early hours, sated with unencumbered lovemaking we began discussing the names: I started: "What about A for a boy, or maybe your Dad's name? G?". And then she returns with:
"I do like A, maybe G if we have another? But what if it is a girl? Your aunt S."
"I'd prefer her to have the more formal D, rather than start out with a shortened nickname."
"Yeah, what about A if he's a boy and D if she's a girl?"
"Done!"

And then A was born, excised on a Monday morning to the strains of El Camarón de las Islas, under the glare of bright shiny lights and the dark-circled eyes of exhausted obstetric practitioners. It was only later that we realised that perhaps D was not yet ready to join our family. Some of our family pressed us to tell them what would the name be had it been a girl. We refused to give way. How could you utter the name of someone into whose spirit the breath of life had not yet been given? It just seemed downright odd! It felt as if the names that we had discussed and chosen, no longer belonged to us as words or labels. Perhaps in our thinking and in our lovemaking, naming these spirits brought them into the universe.

More time passed and very soon we found that A needed the company of a sibling. She fell pregnant again, as easily as the first time and again, in

those early hours, we discussed: "Well, D might yet arrive and I still like your Dad's name G. How about that?"
"Yes, let's do that and if it's a boy, he'll have G and if it's a girl, she'll be D".
"That's settled then. I'm happy about that".

G arrived on a Friday afternoon after an uneventful eight-hour labour under the soft lights of a birthing room. The careful ministrations of a young, capable childless midwife (she had two cats) was both simple and good. No harsh lights for G: his lungs filled the room as he belted out his disapproval and we cherished him and loved him straightaway. And again it seemed that D was not yet ready to join us.

A tidy and simple thought: statistically, the next child should be a girl, but F arrived: our third boy. It was a slightly complicated excision, her second Caesarean. The doctor-magician-technicians advised against any more after this one. I wasn't minded to myself anyway. Our lives had become complicated enough as it was.

And so, where is D now? Is she really in the ether, looking for a way into the troubled and corporeal tangled web of war-torn confusion, economic uncertainty and bounteous, forgiving nature? I cannot say that she'll spring from my loins soon for I am alone and no longer partnered with the mother of my three sons. I am sad and disappointed that D is neither companion to my boys: A, G and F, nor to their mother or, for that matter, me. But, I do think I know her a little; I do harbour the thought that she's out there somewhere, even if we have not yet spoken her name. Maybe she was always S, never D. I might yet find out.

Daniel's story came in when I had nearly finished writing the book and wondered where I might put it and then I realised it belonged in Creativity. By telling the story of his disappointment he finally gets to a place of acceptance and hope at the same time.

I have a beautiful book called Painting the Dream about David Chethlahe Paladin. He was a mixed-race Navajo and an extraordinary man and in the preface it explains that in many traditions there are four common paths: Via Positiva (joy and wonder), Via Negativa (darkness, suffering and silence), Via Creativa (creativity) and Via Transformativa (compassion, healing and justice). How many times have I heard "...but I am not creative"? In my experience that is absolutely not true – creativity is about bringing something in the world that didn't exist before. Changing the form of one thing into another. Our minds can be extraordinarily creative, especially when we are co-creators of our disappointment or fears of being disappointing. If we weren't creative human beings would not exist. Creativity is an outward expression of ourselves and can be an extraordinary tool in helping us see what is hidden and so find a solution. **Creativity can then become a form of mental and emotional recycling....**

Strangely enough, writing a business plan can be just as creative as making a chair out of some old wood. Building a fire is an act of creativity, the list is endless. One thing that creativity does is it focuses our senses and can help us find solutions. Julia Cameron has written one of my favourite books called *The Artist's Way* which is an amazing tool in helping you source your creativity. It isn't necessarily about being an "artist" it is about finding the creator inside you. When all our senses are activated we can always find a solution.

Something very down-to-earth like mind-mapping can be another creative tool. It was devised by Tony Buzan in the late sixties. It is a way of emptying your brain on to paper – apparently randomly – using words, images, numbers and colours, giving your mind the freedom to wander. The magic then happens when you join the information up. Very often this process reveals understanding that you couldn't access before. Using the metaphor of a map this process gives you a surprisingly detailed overview and can enable you to find interesting solutions.

```
            Thought
               |
    ?  ---  Issue  ---  Image
               |
            Thought
```

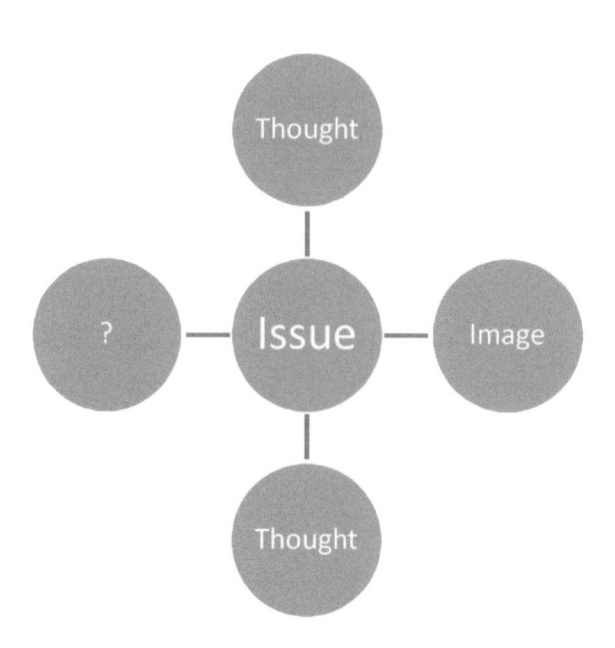

Storytelling is another really healing tool. Being heard, being seen and being understood are fundamental human needs. As the storyteller you allow yourself to become part of the outside world and as the listener you are invited to join in the story if you wish to. Telling someone the story of your disappointment can take away the isolation of being the only person who feels this way. One of the most important questions I was asked after telling a story about a painful incident in my life was "It's understandable to feel that way. How long do you want to feel that way for?". I was seen, I was heard and I was understood but I also saw how I could stay stuck in "my story" and also stay in victim. By telling "the story" to someone we trust can also lead us to finding a way to heal the painful parts of the story. One of the symptoms of being addicted to our story is to tell it to people who will either support us in staying in victim or make us feel inadequate.

How can you use your creative energy to transform the emotional or mental space you are in? Is it by dancing, singing, gardening, carpentry, building things, cooking, sport.....? Or is it by doing something that you have never recognised as being creative before?

Ceremony

Kitty's Story

The feeling of disappointment tends to strike quickly, without warning and I am almost paralysed by the strength of its blow. Before I know it, I am completely detached from myself – find that I almost shut down completely. I battle with trying to justify how strong my feelings are in relation to what "should" be something that I can easily deal with.

The guilt of feeling disappointed in the first instance seems to be the catalyst for an onslaught of fear, loathing, bewilderment and shame! In order to reclaim myself I have to first accept that being disappointed is an acceptable feeling! I need to reinforce my right to feel and allow my experience some truth. I find that until I accept disappointment as a complete emotion I can't move on, as I still fear that the outcome will not change or will bring further disappointment. If I try to move through the emotion too quickly I find that I am still looking for an alternative to the disappointment.

Physically I find that I have to shift. I need to change the energy around me and breathe in a cleansed environment in order to reclaim myself and feel whole again.

Alain de Botton has written an interesting book called *Religion for Atheists* where he talks about the importance of ceremony regardless of our beliefs. His books are very much about a philosophy for life.

We can use all the tools available to help us deal with disappointment but that doesn't take into account maintenance, preventive measures and lessening the impact as Kitty describes it. For me spiritual discipline or regular ceremony is the key to our wellbeing. It's a bit like dusting; just because I dusted on Monday doesn't mean that I won't have to dust on Friday. At least spiritual discipline can be a lot more pleasurable.

Spiritual discipline is very very personal. It can be within a formal religious practice, it can be a ceremony where you plug into the Universe along the lines of Celtic, Buddhist or Native American teachings. It can be part of attending self-help groups particularly 12-Step Programme ones along the lines of Alcoholics Anonymous. Some people's spiritual discipline is quite simply walking the dog and connecting with the world around them, taking a few moments to reflect upon their day. Checking out how they are feeling and if there is anything they need to do or put right that day. Some people journal daily and use that in the same way. Others do Yoga, Tai Chi or some form of physical exercise.

My teachers have all had a message in common – "stay awake" and when my mind is cluttered and my body full of churning feelings, I am fast asleep!

As Kitty says she wants to feel whole. Like Kitty that is what I desire most and disappointment can shatter my energy field very quickly if I don't have that spiritual discipline in place. In some cultures they believe that negative energy can lodge in the cracks of our shattered energy and that this negativity can be passed on throughout the generations to come. There is a lot of research at the moment on epigenetics and how these patterns can evolve and overlay our DNA. A way of healing this is through meditations that take us back through the history of our family DNA and ask that healing light dissolves all the patterns that are no longer of service to us. To begin with it is advisable to do this with someone who understands this process.

This process can also be described as karma. For instance in Nichiren Buddhism there is a teaching that by chanting *'Nam myoho renge kyo'* we can change our karma. In simple terms *'Nam myoho renge kyo'* is the title of the Lotus Sutra and by chanting puts us in rythmn with the Mystic Law of cause and effect bringing us to a place of peace and happiness.

Fasting and pilgrimage are rituals that exist in most spiritual practices and I feel they can be figuratively used in dealing with painful emotions such as disappointment. As I have mentioned before, it is about a willingness to be willing to eventually let go. Fasting could be just for a day in order to let go by visualizing the thoughts and feelings being dissolved into a candle flame or throwing a stone holding all the pain into a river or, best of all, the sea, as the salt is a strong purifier. Chanting mantras each time the thoughts and feelings come into your head - this is not about avoidance but willingness to let go after acknowledgment of the issues. If we use these tools to fast a day at a time the feelings can heal at a very deep level. Just reflecting over our week and checking our feelings connected to events and doing this exercise is great maintenance and doesn't allow issues to grow or begin to hide.

Pilgrimage could be the quest for a sense of resolution. It could be literal such as visiting a place that has a healing energy for you or going there via meditation asking to be given guidance. If it is difficult to visualise you can work with a photograph, music or simply sounds such as the movement of waves, birdsong, etc. Often the answers don't come immediately but afterwards. A slogan on the side of a truck, an overheard random phrase, an advert on a train. When we are willing the Universe will meet us half way. Personally I ask to be shown in three different ways so that I don't go into magical thinking to get the answer I WANT as opposed to the answer I NEED.

I am convinced that some of us have at least one layer of metaphorical skin missing if not more. I certainly do, which is why spiritual discipline is so important to me. I need to be able to acknowledge my shadow as much as the light side of my persona because this gives me an awareness of my conscience. Without our shadow we might become "so heavenly" we would be of no earthly good.

For me I like to describe it as maintaining my plumbing and electrical circuits mentally and emotionally. When I understood that I really don't want to leak, flood or have burst pipes and certainly not blow fuses or set fire to myself – I was motivated. I happen to like rituals, so in the morning I have a simple routine that enables me to clean off my energy field by having a very quick cold shower; apparently negative energy hates cold water which makes sense to me as fungi thrive in dark dank warm places. Sometimes it is literally a splash. I have a little twirl to shake my body back into alignment and then I do some Chi Kung exercises. After that I meditate usually by chanting and reflect on my day. I also hand over all my loved ones and clients to the Universe and ask to do the best I can.

I have been doing this for a long time and it works for me. It has also taught me that if I struggle with certain people I can be grateful to them because they are GOOD enemies and teach me something I need to learn or readjust in my thinking. It has also taught me to stay in a process even if everything appears to be going wrong because it might be taking me to a better place in the end. Lastly, part of my spiritual discipline is to have a laughter kit full of books, films, pictures that make me laugh because I don't know when I am going to need it. Michael with John Travolta playing the Archangel Michael who is sent down to Earth still works for me.

Quite a few years ago I was in the depth of despair about something and I was alone at home pacing round the house, up the stairs and back again feeling more and more trapped by my overwhelming emotions. I got to the point that I had lost all sense of what I was doing and accidentally I put the television on and there was a Bill Cosby show on and for a moment I was about to laugh. I was so obsessed with the negativity that I heard myself say to myself "you can't possibly laugh. You are in so much pain for heaven's sake", but the television kept catching my attention and finally I sat down and watched the programme and laughed myself better. As Kitty says I need to allow myself my feelings but I can also recover from them.

I am continuously devising new forms of meditations which clients and friends are finding extremely useful as they are mainly in the form of short audios. They can be found on my websites www.tiegsolus.moonfruit.com and www.chloeaspreyblog.com.

What is your practice, your ceremony?

Stress Management

Disappointment, because of all the different emotions and responses it can evoke, creates an enormous amount of stress in our being. Stress management can be used proactively as well as a tool to restabilise after the effects of disappointment. Sometimes stress is caused by one traumatic event and at other times it can be cumulative as a result of lots of little disappointments beginning to cluster together.

Below are some tools that you might find useful together with a checklist of symptoms to ascertain whether you might need some professional support.

Stopping: Say STOP to yourself out loud if possible. Change your body position e.g. if you are standing, sit down. Don't take on any further commitments – in the case of disappointment this might mean walk away and take time to reflect.

Reflection/Relaxation: Meditation, mindfulness exercises, Reiki, gentle breathing, humour. Always choose something that is relaxing for you.

Freeing Attention Outward: Ask yourself "what is going on right now?", "what choices do I have?". Remember that Fear can stand for False Evidence Appearing Real.

Change your Time Perspective: "How long is this feeling actually going to last?". Take a reality check with someone else. Watch out for "this is how it was, this is how it is, and this is how it always will be". Do your best to stay in the present.

Balancing and Recognising Constraints: Look at what you can and can't change realistically. Readjust your expectations; reaffirm your limitations especially around boundaries with other people. Ask yourself "where's the fire?", "who is cracking the whip?" "am I dancing to someone else's tune?".

Use your Support Network: Don't isolate with the problem, the feelings. Speak to people you trust and if this is an issue begin to do your best to build up a network.

Diet and Exercise: Make sure that your diet is balanced. Too much sugar and eating too little can make us hypersensitive as well as too much alcohol and certain drugs. A balanced amount of exercise so that you oxygenate your body. Lack of fresh air or too much exercise can also make us hypersensitive.

Characteristics of Negative Coping Strategies
- Preoccupation (obsessive thinking)
- Isolation (alone with the feelings, problems)
- Taking addictive substances, eating inappropriately to relieve stress
- Denial of the problem, feelings (maximising or minimising)
- Staying in the problem, feelings - talking about this all the time
- Loss of control – the situation takes over your life
- Higher capacity than others ("I don't know how you manage")
- Loss of memory – particularly short-term

Physical Symptoms
- Insomnia
- Short Circuit Anger
- Irrational Crying
- Poor immune system
- Minor injuries on a regular basis
- Skin problems

- Irritability
- Headaches
- Muscular pain
- Food allergies, digestive problems
- Nervous system problems

A good rule of thumb is if you have three or more of these symptoms, you may need some professional help or become part of a self-help group like one of the 12-Step Programmes based on the principles of Alcoholics Anonymous.

Children

I would like to end the book with a chapter about children. I woke up the other morning with the question "How do we protect the children?". This question then led me to reflect on how much are we responsible for clouding their dreams, hopes and expectations.

Being over-protective, by projecting our own fears and disappointments, can be counterproductive and simply reinforces negative strategies and beliefs. Somehow it wouldn't feel right to control our children's feelings or to prevent them from feeling disappointed or experience disappointments. What we can do is be aware of their individual responses to different situations and support them in finding a way through the experiences.

We all have different personalities and have different responses to the same situations. One of the reasons I was motivated to write this book is that I saw what happened to one of my grandchildren when someone said they were disappointed in him. His instant physical response mirrored shame, confusion, hurt and rebellion at the same time. His body then literally crumpled. His brother would probably appear not to be affected. I have used the word "probably" on purpose as these responses can be deeply buried. One brother outwardly showing his feelings and the other one doing the opposite. Of course, there is also the possibility, depending on the circumstances, that there is no lasting response. As adults what we can do is take more care with our language and observation skills.

Children spend a huge part of their childhood at school and the principles laid down by Maria Montessori are inspiring for anyone who has care of children:

"Children are individuals profoundly affected by society and the immediate environment. Every child is born with creative potential, the drive to learn and the right to be treated as an individual.

Specially prepared environments, in school and at home, help to develop the child's natural potential.

Children must be given freedom to work and move around within suitable guidelines that enable them to act as part of a social group.

Children should be provided with specifically designed materials which help them to explore their world and enable them to develop essential cognitive skills.

Mixed age groups encourage all children to develop their personalities socially and intellectually at their own pace."

These principles are mirrored in many cultures including "specifically designed materials", although in Bedouin tribes they may take the shape of a herd of camels. Young children are often given a camel to take care of and in this way their self-worth is nurtured as their community depends on these animals in many different ways. The Aboriginal grandmothers followed these principles in the healing process of the "lost" children in their communities.

We are living in exciting times where there are many opportunities to heal the things that disturb us and those who have remained connected to some of the old effective ways of healing are willing to share their wisdom again. The combination of modern science and ancient teachings are being investigated and experts from different sides of the various philosophies are beginning to talk to each other instead of insisting that "my way is the right way".
There may be times when a father or mother can't make Sports Day, a special concert or event. There may be times when a child feels they haven't got the results they hoped for. There may be times when they rush home full of enthusiasm about something they did

at school and somehow it falls flat when they try to share it at home. Teenagers can feel under a lot of pressure to meet all sorts of expectations, their own and other people's and can become vulnerable enough to commit suicide. In my therapy practice, I am seeing more and more teenagers and am encouraged that more and more frequently they willingly have a desire to find solutions to their disappointments.

There are no magic solutions but, in my practice as a therapist, the common thread is that we all need to be seen, heard and valued for who we are, not for who other people want us to be or for who we think we "should" be. This is also about balance and learning how to manage our feelings. Timing is perhaps after all a magic key, putting aside time to talk and hear each other's points of view, it doesn't matter how old we are. In my heart of hearts I have written this book for my grandchildren and the generations to come as I passionately believe in the possibility of peace and not allowing bitterness and disappointment to continually lead us into conflict.

The child in all of us will usually respond to storytelling, one of the most ancient teaching tools. I wrote the story of "Bear and how he learned to take care of himself" for all of us. We all forget at times in order to remember....

BEAR – how he learned to take care of himself.

Bear was walking along feeling really miserable. He felt as if he had this big black cloud looming over him. He had his head down, his eyes on his feet. Suddenly he noticed there was a little frog in front of him.

"Hallo" said Frog. "Hallo" said Bear.

"How are you feeling today?" asked Frog. "Well I feel miserable. I have felt miserable for a long time. In fact I don't really want to be here at all" replied Bear.

"Oh!" said Frog. "Do you think it might have something to do with that big black cloud hanging over your head?" he asked.

"It might" said Bear. "Well I might know somewhere that might be able to help you. Do you want to come and see?" asked Frog. "Alright" grumped Bear.

So along they went. Frog hopping, Bear trudging. Finally Frog stopped and said "Look, why don't you go and stand under that waterfall? It will be a bit cold, but I guarantee you will feel a bit better".

Still grumping, Bear stepped under the waterfall. It was only for a second as it really was very cold. He tingled all over and had the strangest feeling he had been kissed by an angel! "Hmmm" he thought "I do feel a bit better". Sooo he said goodbye to the frog and carried on walking.

"Flit, flit" he heard and realised a beautiful butterfly was whirling around him, finally landing on his shoulder and whispered into his ear "I know you feel a bit better since you went under the waterfall but you would feel a thousand times better if you just did a little whirl with me".

"A little whirl?" said Bear with an edge of grump still there. "Yes" said the butterfly. "A little whirl. Just try and catch me". And the butterfly whirled around Bear and Bear tried to catch it until he found himself whirling and whirling. All of a sudden the butterfly vanished and Bear suddenly stopped. He felt a little dizzy to begin with but when he became more balanced, he did indeed feel a thousand times better!

"Goodness me, I do, I really do feel better. I wonder why?". Then he saw all sorts of jagged bits, sticky bits and lumpy bits on the ground at his feet which must have fallen out of his fur. They all had depressing messages attached to them. He noticed that the earth was just absorbing them and then transforming them into beautiful petals. He carried on walking feeling so much lighter. Then he caught sight of a beautiful multi-coloured flower. He had never seen one like this before. He stopped, bent down to smell it and as he did that he noticed that he became surrounded by a rainbow egg. When he straightened up he could see that everything around him sparkled with light. "Wow! This is where I live. It has always been like this but I just haven't noticed for such a long time" he thought with a mixture of wonder and sadness. He sighed with contentment and gratitude and decided to sit down for a while. As he looked around him, he began to remember the things his mother had told him when he was little. Teaching him to look after his rainbow egg with cold water and whirling and then filling it with rainbow light. How could he have forgotten?

Then he remembered her showing him how to do exercises to keep his body happy. One of them was called Salute the Sun and some others were called Chi Kung. He wanted to do one right then and there and decided to Salute the Sun. He could feel himself becoming stronger and taller; really connected to the world around him as if he had literally plugged himself into the Universe, making sure his feet were firmly on the earth beneath him.

But he wondered again about the black cloud and amongst the jagged bits he had noticed there were worries about the future and other people. Then he got a fantastic idea: he could put them all into a beautiful boat and push it into an ocean of healing water asking that the Universe take care of them all. He was so excited that he went round saying thank you to absolutely everything in his bright new world, to all the plants, animals and humans as well as the minerals, the sun, the moon, the stars – absolutely everything.

Finally he understood that he had had to feel the black cloud and being miserable so that he would really want to look after himself. He never wanted to forget again and so he went off in search of other grumpy bears so that he could help them too and share his experiences. Off down the path he went but he wasn't alone because hopping along and flitting around him were Frog and Butterfly just in case he needed some company and maybe a little help.